How to Handle "I'm Just Looking" in Car Sales

A Simple System to Turn Brush-Offs into Productive Conversations

Bruce Huddleston

Bedrock Heritage Publishing

ISBN: 978-1-972179-26-0

EPUB: 978-1-972179-60-4

Manufactured in the United States of America

Bedrock Heritage Publishing

Tyler, Texas

www.bedrockheritagepublishing.com

info@bedrockheritagepublishing.com

www.carsalessurvivalseries.com

DISCLAIMER

This book is based on the author's personal and professional experiences, observations, and opinions accumulated over a thirty-five-year career in the automotive industry. It is intended for educational and informational purposes only.

The stories and anecdotes contained in this book are drawn from real-world situations encountered throughout the author's career. However, names, identifying details, specific circumstances, employer names, dealership names, and individual characteristics have been changed, omitted, combined, or fictionalized to protect the privacy of the individuals involved. Any resemblance to specific living persons, current or former employers, or existing businesses is coincidental and unintentional.

No individual, dealership, organization, or employer referenced or implied in the stories within this book has reviewed, approved, or endorsed the content herein. The recollections and characterizations presented are solely the author's own perspective and memory of events and do not constitute a factual record, legal testimony, or statement of fact regarding any identifiable person or entity.

The sales strategies, techniques, and professional advice presented in this book reflect the author's personal approach and experience. Individual results will vary based on experience, effort, market conditions, dealership policies, and other factors beyond the author's control. Nothing in this book constitutes a guarantee of income, employment, or professional outcome.

The author and publisher have made reasonable efforts to ensure the accuracy of information presented at the time of writing. The author and publisher make no representations or warranties regarding the completeness, accuracy, or current applicability of the information contained herein, and expressly disclaim any liability arising from the use or application of the content of this book.

By reading this book, you acknowledge and agree that the author and publisher shall not be liable for any damages, losses, or claims arising directly or indirectly from the use of or reliance upon any information contained herein.

DEDICATION

To the salespeople who have ever stood on a lot, heard "I'm just looking," and
felt the air go out of them.
This book is for you.
That phrase is not the end. It never was. You just needed someone to show
you what to do next.
— Bruce Huddleston

FREE BONUS FOR READERS

Your Complete Digital Script Library

Thank you for reading How to Handle "I'm Just Looking" in Car Sales.

As a reader, you have access to a free companion resource: The "I'm Just Looking" Quick Reference Card — a one-page summary of the core system in this book, formatted for easy review before a shift or sales meeting.

To download your free copy, visit:
www.carsalessurvivalseries.com/scripts
Enter your email to claim your free reader bonus.

CONTENTS

INTRODUCTION

Why "I'm Just Looking" Is the Most Important Phrase in Car Sales

Every salesperson in this business has heard it.

You walk out. You introduce yourself. You smile, you extend a hand, you do everything right — and the customer looks at you and says, "I'm just looking."

And just like that, the air goes out of it.

Most new salespeople hear that phrase as a door closing. They back off, they disappear, they tell themselves the customer wasn't serious. Some of them go back inside and watch from the window, waiting for a signal that never comes.

Here is what I want you to understand before we get into anything else:

"I'm just looking" is not a no. It is not a rejection. It is not even close to the end of the conversation.

It is the beginning of one.

I spent 35 years on dealership floors—selling, managing, training. I have heard that phrase more times than I can count. And I can tell you without any hesitation that some of the best deals I ever saw started with a customer saying they were just looking.

The phrase is a reflex. Customers say it because they've been burned before. They've walked onto a lot and had someone in dress clothes sprint at them from fifty yards away. They've been cornered, pressured, and worn down. So they put the phrase up like a shield before any of that can happen.

That shield is not aimed at you. It is aimed at the situation.

When you learn to handle those three words correctly — calmly, confidently, without flinching — you become a different kind of salesperson. You stop losing deals in the first thirty seconds. You start having actual conversations. And those conversations lead where conversations are supposed to lead.

This book is a system. Not a script you memorize and recite. A system — something you understand deeply enough that you can use it in any situation, with any customer type, in any condition on the lot.

We are going to cover what the phrase actually means, why customers say it, what mistakes salespeople make when they hear it, and what you do instead. We will go through responses that work, body language you need to read, and the full repeatable process for turning a brush-off into a conversation.

By the end of this book, "I'm just looking" will not bother you anymore. It will tell you exactly what to do next.

"The Rule: 'I'm just looking' is not rejection. It is information. Your job is to respond to it — not react to it."

Chapter 1

What Customers Really Mean When They Say It

L ET'S START WITH THE truth.

When a customer says, "I'm just looking," they are seldom telling you they don't want to buy a car.

Most of the time, they are telling you one of four things.

They want a minute to breathe.

Customers pull onto a lot, and they've already got their guard up. They've heard the stories. Maybe they've lived the stories. High pressure, no breathing room, someone following them around the lot before they even got both feet out of the car. So the minute they see you walking toward them, the phrase comes out. It's automatic. It doesn't mean anything about you specifically. It means they don't know you yet, and they want a few seconds to get their feet under them.

They don't know what they want yet.

Many customers come in without a clear picture. They know they need something. They know roughly what they can spend. But they haven't decided on a model, a body style, or whether they want a new or used vehicle. "I'm just looking" is sometimes just an honest statement: they are looking.

They haven't narrowed it down. Give them a minute, and they'll start asking questions.

They got there too fast.

You approached before they were ready. That happens. It's not a disaster. They stepped out, they hadn't even closed the car door, and there you were. The phrase is a way of pumping the brakes. It doesn't mean they're leaving. It means they want to slow the pace down.

It's got nothing to do with you or the car.

Sometimes something else is entirely going on. Something personal. Something situational. Something about the day they've had, who they're with, how that whole morning went. I have seen customers say they were just looking and then buy a vehicle forty-five minutes later once the right person showed up in front of them. We'll talk about that more in Chapter 8.

The point is this: you can't know which one it is in the first five seconds. And if you assume it's rejection, you will lose deals that were never lost.

New salespeople make that mistake constantly. They hear the phrase, they interpret it as a verdict, and they fold. They go back inside. They give the customer nothing to work with.

Experienced salespeople hear the phrase and think: okay. Now, what does this person actually need from me right now?

That is the question this whole book is built around.

"The Rule: Don't interpret. Don't assume. Listen to what the phrase is actually telling you and respond to that."

CHAPTER 2

WHY SALESPEOPLE GET IT WRONG

I F "I'M JUST LOOKING" is so easy to misread, why do so many salespeople misread it?

Because they've been trained wrong, or they haven't been trained at all. Or they've absorbed bad habits from watching others handle it poorly.

Here is what I see most often.

They take it personally.

The customer says, "I'm just looking," and the salesperson hears: You specifically are not someone I want to talk to. That's not what the customer said. That's what the salesperson's ego heard. Once you make it personal, you've already lost your objectivity. You start reacting instead of responding. That's when the wheels come off.

They push back.

Some salespeople hear the brush-off and immediately try to power through it. "Well, let me just show you what we've got." "We've actually got a great special running this weekend." They keep going like the customer never said anything. That doesn't work. The customer said they needed space. The salesperson just proved they weren't listening. Now the walls go up higher.

They disappear.

The other extreme. They say "sure" and walk back inside, and that is the last the customer sees of them—no presence on the lot. No availability.

Nothing. The customer eventually has a question, but there's no one there, so they get back in their car and drive somewhere else. The salesperson calls it a lost cause. It wasn't. They just weren't there when the moment came.

They talk too much.

The customer says they're just looking, and the salesperson launches into a monologue. Features, inventory, weekend specials, financing options, and certified pre-owned programs. The customer didn't ask for any of that. They asked for a minute. Instead, they got buried. Now they have to physically escape to get the space they already said they needed.

They give up and start prospecting the lot instead.

I have watched salespeople get the brush-off from one customer and immediately turn around to scan for another. They've already written off the person standing right in front of them. Meanwhile, that first customer wanders the lot alone, forms a few impressions, and leaves because no one comes back.

Every one of these mistakes has the same root cause.

The salesperson made a decision about the customer based on three words.

Three words. That's all the information they had. And they used it to write off what could have been a deal.

The system in this book is designed to interrupt that pattern. You are going to learn to hold your response, read the situation more carefully, and give the customer what they actually need in that moment — which is usually a lot simpler than you think.

"The Rule: The most expensive mistake in car sales is making decisions about customers with almost no information. Hold off. Watch. Respond to what you actually see."

CHAPTER 3

THE PSYCHOLOGY OF THE BRUSH-OFF

L ET'S TALK ABOUT WHAT is actually happening when a customer says, "I'm just looking."

Not what they say. What is happening underneath it?

Buying a car is not like buying a cup of coffee. It is one of the largest financial decisions most people make. It involves trade-in value, financing, insurance, payment structure, and a vehicle they are going to live with for years. The stakes are real. And dealerships have long had a reputation — fair or not — for making that process feel adversarial.

So customers arrive in a defensive posture. That's not paranoia. That's self-protection. They have an instinct to maintain control of the situation, and the fastest way to do that when someone approaches them is to establish distance. "I'm just looking." Is that the distance? It is a boundary.

Here is what matters: a boundary is not a wall. It is a request. The customer is saying, "I need to feel safe before this conversation goes anywhere." Give me a moment to assess things.

Salespeople who understand this respond to the request rather than treating it as an obstacle to push through.

Control is the keyword.

Customers want to feel like they are driving the process. The minute they feel like the process is being done to them — the pressure, the urgency, the closing technique coming at them before they've even decided what they want — they shut down. Some of them leave.

When you respond to "I'm just looking" in a way that gives the customer back control, something shifts. The tension drops. The guard comes down. Not all the way or immediately, but it's starting to move in the right direction.

That is the whole game at this stage. Not closing, not presenting, not asking qualifying questions, just getting the temperature down enough that a real conversation becomes possible.

The expectation gap.

Most customers expect to be pressured. They've braced for it. So when you don't pressure them — when you are calm, professional, and give them actual space — it surprises them. And that surprise works in your favor.

Suddenly, you are not the salesperson they were dreading. You are someone different. Someone who might actually be worth talking to.

That is a significant advantage. And you created it simply by not doing what they expected you to do.

Time is not your enemy.

New salespeople treat every second of silence like a failure. The customer isn't talking, so something must be wrong, so they fill the space. That is almost always a mistake.

Give the customer room to move around. Let them look. Let the lot do some of the work. A customer who has a few minutes to walk around without pressure starts to relax. And a relaxed customer is an open customer.

You are not wasting time. You are making the deal possible.

"The Rule: The customer's guard is not the enemy of the sale. It's the gate to it. Respond correctly, and it opens. Push against it, and it locks."

CHAPTER 4

THE FIRST RESPONSE THAT KEEPS THE DOOR OPEN

EVERYTHING WE HAVE COVERED so far leads to this.

What do you actually say when a customer says, "I'm just looking"?

The answer is simpler than most people expect, which is probably why so many people get it wrong. They are looking for something clever. Something that shows off their training. Something that counters the brush-off with a little verbal judo.

That is not what works. What works is this:

FROM THE FLOOR

One afternoon, a customer pulled into the lot in a taxi. That caught my attention — most people drive themselves in. This one stepped out and walked directly toward a specific vehicle, as if he already knew exactly what he was looking for.

I didn't rush. I stood up, walked out at a normal pace, and gave him a small wave as I crossed the lot. When I reached him, I introduced myself and told him I'd be glad to help if he had any questions.

He told me he'd just gotten off a flight and came straight from the airport. His vehicle was destroyed in a parking lot fire while he was traveling. He'd seen one of our ads and came directly to us. He knew which vehicle he wanted. He just needed to drive it and confirm it.

We took a short test drive. Came back. He asked how to make out the check.

Start to finish, maybe forty-five minutes. The deal was easy because the approach was right. No pressure, no assumptions, no rushing. Just a professional greeting and a willingness to follow the customer's lead.

Not every customer comes in ready to buy. But every customer deserves that same professional opening. You never know which one is going to be the taxi customer — the one who's already decided and just needs someone not to get in their way.

That story is not about a special situation. It is about what every situation should look like.

The taxi customer did not say, "I'm just looking." But if he had, the approach would have been exactly the same. Calm. Normal pace. No assumptions. A professional introduction and an offer to help.

Here is the formula. Three parts. Simple.

1. Acknowledge without caving.

When the customer says they're just looking, do not apologize for approaching. Do not act like you did something wrong. Say something that confirms you heard them and that you are completely fine with it.

"No problem at all. Take your time."

That's it. Relaxed. No edge to it. No subtext. You heard them, and you respect what they said.

2. Stay present.

You are not disappearing. You are not going back inside. You are in the general area, available, doing whatever looks natural—checking a nearby vehicle, straightening something, just being on the lot. The customer can see you. They know where you are. That matters. When they have a question, there will be someone to ask.

3. Leave the door open.

Before you step back, give them a low-pressure invitation—just one. No closing. Just a door left open.

"If anything catches your eye and you want to take a look inside or take something for a drive, just let me know."

That's not a pitch. That's permission. You just told the customer that when they're ready — on their schedule, in their own time — you are available to help. There is no pressure in that sentence. And that's exactly why it works.

The whole exchange takes about fifteen seconds. And in those fifteen seconds, you have completely separated yourself from every salesperson the customer was dreading.

You did not push. You did not disappear. You acknowledged, you stayed present, and you left the door open.

Now you wait. Not forever. We will talk about timing in the next few chapters. But for right now, you have done your job. The customer knows you are there. The ball is in their court.

Most of the time, they will come to you.

"The Rule: Acknowledge. Stay. Leave the door open. That's the whole first response. Do not overthink it."

CHAPTER 5

GIVING SPACE WITHOUT DISAPPEARING

THERE IS A VERSION of "give them space" that ends the deal.

You back off, go inside, sit down, and get a cup of coffee. The customer is alone on the lot. Nobody is checking on them. Nobody nearby. They walk around for a few minutes, look at two or three vehicles, and then they get in their car and drive away. Maybe they'll come back. Probably they won't.

That is not giving space. That is abandoning the lot.

Giving space correctly means you are still present. You are visible. You are accessible. The customer can find you in five seconds if they want to. You are just not hovering over them while they think.

The difference sounds small. It is not small. It is often the difference between a deal and an empty lot.

What presence on the lot actually looks like.

You are not standing ten feet behind the customer, staring at them. You are not watching from inside through the window. You are on the lot, doing something that looks natural — checking a vehicle, straightening something, walking a different section. Close enough for them to see you. Far enough that they don't feel monitored.

This takes a little practice. New salespeople tend toward one extreme or the other — either shadowing the customer like a security guard or disappearing completely — neither works. You want to find the middle: present, calm, unhurried.

Think about how a good server works in a restaurant. They are not standing at your elbow while you read the menu. But they are not hiding in the kitchen either. They are in the room, visible, available, ready when you look up. That is the energy you want on the lot.

The natural check-in.

After a few minutes — and how many minutes depends on what you see from the customer, which we will cover in the next chapter — it is appropriate to drift back toward them and check in. Not with a sales question. With something easy.

"You finding everything okay?"

"Anything you'd like me to grab the keys for?"

"If you want to sit inside any of these, just say the word."

That's not pressure. That's a door. You are reminding them you are there, offering something useful, and doing so without any urgency. Most customers will either take you up on it or say "no thanks, still looking"—and both are fine. The second one just means you step back again and give them a little more time.

What you are communicating without saying it.

When you stay present without hovering, you communicate a few things the customer needs to feel.

You are not desperate. A desperate salesperson shadows every customer, afraid of losing the deal. A confident salesperson knows the deal is still there as long as they handle it right. That confidence reads. Customers feel it.

You are a professional. You showed up, you gave a good first response, and now you are managing the situation like someone who has done this before. That matters to a customer who came in braced for chaos.

You are trustworthy. This is the quietest one, but probably the most important. A customer who feels watched or pressured does not trust the person watching them. A customer who is given real space and treated like an adult starts to build a little trust. Not a lot yet. But enough to start talking.

All of that happens without you saying a word, by being present in the right way.

"The Rule: Stay on the lot. Stay visible. Stay calm. The customer gave you nothing to work with yet — don't give them a reason to leave before they do."

CHAPTER 6

THE FOLLOW-UP THAT DOESN'T FEEL LIKE A FOLLOW-UP

THERE IS A MOMENT, somewhere between the brush-off and the sale, where the salesperson has to re-enter the conversation.

Most salespeople blow it.

They wait too long, and the customer is already leaving. Or they come back too soon, and the customer feels like the space they asked for wasn't real. Or they come back with the wrong energy — pushy, overeager, clearly trying to move the process forward — and the customer shuts down again.

The follow-up that works does not feel like a follow-up. It feels like a natural moment in a conversation that was never really interrupted.

Timing.

There is no universal number. Three minutes. Five minutes. It depends on what the customer is doing. If they are moving quickly around the lot, barely pausing, they are still orienting. Give them more time. If they have slowed down and are spending real time on a specific vehicle — walking around it, looking in the windows, reading the sticker — that is your signal. They have found something. That is when you move.

You do not need a dramatic entrance. You walk over naturally, like you happened to be in that direction. You glance at the vehicle they're looking at.

"That's a solid one."

That's it. Three words. You are not pitching. You are not launching into a features presentation. You are just acknowledging what they are already interested in. You are joining the conversation they are already having in their head.

Transition questions that open the door.

Once you are standing next to them and the ice is slightly broken, the follow-up question is simple. You want to find out what they are actually thinking without making them feel interrogated.

"Is this the size you're looking for, or are you still deciding?"

"Do you want to take a look inside?"

"Are you replacing something, or is this more of a change-up?"

These questions are easy to answer. They require almost no commitment. And every answer gives you information — information you are going to need to help them find the right vehicle.

The customer who says, "I'm replacing my truck, it's got 180,000 miles on it," just opened a real conversation. You did not push them there. You just made it easy for them to walk through the door.

What not to do.

Do not come back with a close. "So what would it take to put you in this one today?" That is not a follow-up. That is a threat. The customer just asked for space, and now you are asking for a commitment. You have not earned that yet. Do not jump to it.

Do not come back with inventory information they did not ask for. "We've got three of these in stock, two in different colors, and there's a special financing rate this month." You just turned a quiet moment into a sales pitch. The customer will feel it and back off again.

Come back with something small. Something natural. A comment about what they are looking at. A question that is easy to answer. Let them lead for the next 30 seconds, and you follow.

That is the follow-up that does not feel like one.

"The Rule: Re-enter the conversation the way a good friend would — by joining where the customer already is, not by dragging them somewhere they didn't ask to go."

CHAPTER 7

READING THE CUSTOMER WHILE THEY BROWSE

WHILE THE CUSTOMER IS on the lot and you are giving them space, you are not idle.

You are watching.

Not in a creepy way. Not standing there with your arms crossed, studying them, but paying attention. Because the customer is telling you things right now — things they haven't said out loud yet — and if you know how to read them, you will know exactly when and how to come back.

Where do they go first?

The first vehicle a customer walks toward is rarely random. They may not know specifically what they want, but their feet usually take them somewhere with a reason. A truck section. A row of SUVs. The used inventory rather than new. Pay attention to that first move.

If they head straight for something specific, they have probably already been doing research. They know more than they're letting on. That changes your approach when you re-engage. You can skip the basics and meet them a little further down the road.

How they move.

A customer who moves quickly — glancing at vehicles, not stopping — is still in the early orientation phase. They are getting a feel for the lot. That is fine. Give them room.

A customer who slows down, circles a vehicle, touches the door handle, or crouches to look at the wheel wells is making an evaluation. They are not just looking anymore. They are interested. That is your signal that the window is opening.

The speed of their movement will tell you almost exactly how ready they are to talk.

Body language signals that the door is opening.

They look up from the vehicle and glance in your direction. That is not accidental. They are checking whether you are available. Move toward them.

They stop moving and stand next to a vehicle for more than thirty seconds. They are thinking about it. That is the moment to drift over with something easy.

They try the door handle. They want to look inside. If you have the key or can get it, this is a natural opening: "Want to take a look inside? I can grab the key."

They look at the window sticker and then look around. They have a question, and they are deciding whether to ask it. Be close enough to be the obvious person to ask.

Body language signals that say not yet.

They are still moving, still walking, still scanning. Let them.

They are engaged in conversation with someone they brought with them. Let them talk. That conversation is part of their process. Your interruption may not be welcome.

They have their back to you, and they have not looked back once. Give them more time.

Eyes down, moving fast, not pausing: they are not ready. Do not approach. Wait.

The face gives it away.

Watch for the moment the expression changes. A customer who is browsing with a neutral face, then pauses, and their expression shifts — they see something, something connects — that is the moment. That face will tell you before any of their words will.

This is a skill that builds over time. But you can start developing it right now just by paying attention instead of looking at your phone while customers are on the lot.

The lot is always telling you something. You just have to be watching.

"The Rule: The customer's feet, pace, hands, and eyes will tell you when the door is open. Watch for the signals and respond to them — not to a timer."

CHAPTER 8

WHEN "I'M JUST LOOKING" IS REALLY ABOUT YOU

MOST OF THE TIME, "I'm just looking" has nothing to do with you personally. It is a reflex. A habit. A wall that the customer puts up before they know who they are dealing with.

But sometimes it is about you.

Not because you did something wrong. Not because you said the wrong thing or had the wrong energy. Sometimes the issue is something you cannot see or change—and knowing that is one of the most important things in this business.

FROM THE FLOOR

I had a colleague who couldn't get any traction with a woman at the used-car lot. She kept saying she was just looking. He couldn't figure out what was off — he'd done everything right as far as he could tell. He came and got me.

I went out, introduced myself, and asked how I could help her.

She said, "Thank God you're here. I really want to buy this car. But that other guy looks exactly like my ex-husband, and I cannot stand the sight of him."

Nothing to do with the car. Nothing to do with the approach. She knew exactly what she wanted — she just needed a different person in front of her before she was going to let the conversation happen. We tested the vehicle, worked out fair numbers, and she drove home happy.

Don't take "I'm just looking" personally. Don't take it as a verdict. Take it as information — something needs to be adjusted. Sometimes that's your approach. Sometimes it's giving more space. And occasionally it's a different person entirely. All of those are workable. None of them is the end of the deal.

That story is not unusual. It happens more often than people want to admit.

The lesson is not that you failed. The lesson is that sometimes the obstacle between a customer and a sale is invisible to you and has nothing to do with anything you did. When you understand that, you stop taking the brush-off personally. You start treating it as a problem to be solved rather than a verdict to accept.

How to know when it might be you.

You have given the customer space. You have done the right follow-up. You have read their body language, and the signals all said they were ready to talk. But every time you approach, the wall goes back up. They are not leaving—they are still on the lot, still interested in the vehicle—but something is not connecting between you.

That is the moment to consider whether a turn would better serve the customer.

The mandatory turn.

Most professional dealerships have a system for this. A turn is when one salesperson passes a customer to another. It happens for many reasons, and it is not a sign of failure. It is a sign of professionalism. The goal is to get the customer what they need, not to protect any one salesperson's pride.

When you bring in a partner on a turn, you do it without drama. You do not tell them everything the customer said. You do not prejudge the situation. The new salesperson starts fresh — new introduction, clean slate, no baggage from the first interaction.

And here is the most important thing: if you are the salesperson getting the turn, you do not assume anything. You walk out as if it's the first time anyone has spoken to this customer. Because sometimes it effectively is.

What this story teaches about the whole system.

The Ex-Husband story is the extreme version. But the principle applies broadly.

Sometimes a customer says, "I'm just looking," and there is an obstacle you cannot see. Maybe they had a terrible experience at another dealership that morning. Maybe they got bad news on the way over. Maybe they just have a personality that takes longer to warm up to certain kinds of energy.

None of that is your fault. All of it is workable. You adjust. You give more space, bring someone else in, or just slow everything way down and let the customer set the entire pace.

The professional does not let their ego get in the way of the deal. They ask: What does this customer need right now? And then they provide it—even if what they need is someone else.

"The Rule: Sometimes the obstacle is invisible. When the customer is still on the lot, but the conversation keeps stalling, ask yourself what needs to change — not whether you should give up."

C H A P T E R 9

Turning the Browse into a Conversation

A T SOME POINT, THE browse has to become something more.

The customer has been on the lot. You have given them space. You have read their signals. You came back in at the right moment with something easy, and they responded. Now there is a real opening — a small one, but real — and what you do with it determines whether this becomes a conversation or whether the customer smiles, says thanks, and drives away.

This is the transition. And most salespeople rush it.

They feel the opening, and they immediately try to move the process forward. Qualifying questions, inventory talk, and payments. The customer warmed up a degree, and the salesperson is already trying to put them in the finance office. It does not work. The temperature drops back down, and you are starting over.

The transition from browse to conversation is not a gear change. It is a continuation. You are doing the same thing you have been doing — following the customer's lead, staying calm, not pushing — you are just doing it in dialogue now instead of from a distance.

Start with what they are already looking at.

You walked over because they slowed down on a specific vehicle. That vehicle is your starting point. Not your inventory system. Not your lot map. That vehicle right there.

"This one's been popular. What caught your eye about it?"

That question does three things. It affirms their choice without being pushy about it. It invites them to talk. And it gives you the single most useful piece of information you can have right now: what they actually care about.

Let them answer. Do not talk over the answer or pivot away from it. Whatever they say — the color, the size, the price on the sticker, the fact that it looks like what their neighbor drives — that is your thread. Follow it.

Ask one question at a time.

New salespeople, once they feel the conversation is opening, sometimes unload all their qualifying questions at once. What are you trading? What's your payment range? How soon are you looking to buy? Are you financing or paying cash?

That is an interrogation. The customer was not ready for it, and now they feel like they stepped into something they didn't agree to.

One question. Get the answer. Let that answer take you somewhere. Ask the next question from there. The conversation builds naturally when you let it. It collapses when you force it.

Make it about them, not about the vehicle.

This sounds obvious. It is not obvious to many salespeople.

The salesperson's instinct is to talk about the vehicle's features, specs, and what makes it a good deal. The customer's need is to feel like someone is trying to understand them. Those are not the same thing.

When you ask about their life — what they use a vehicle for, whether they have a long commute, whether they haul anything, whether there are kids involved — you are not stalling. You are doing the most important work in the whole process. You are learning what they actually need, so you can actually help them find it.

Customers who feel understood buy—customers who feel pitched at leave.

Let the conversation meander a little.

Not every sentence has to move the deal forward. If the customer says something about their old truck that leads to a story about a road trip they took, let it breathe. Ask a follow-up. Laugh if it's funny. Be a person.

Sales is a relationship—even a short one. A customer who has had a real conversation with you — even five minutes of one — trusts you more than a customer who has only been presented to. That trust is what makes the rest of the process work.

The browse became a conversation. The conversation will become a sale. Not by forcing it — by following it.

"The Rule: The conversation is the sale. When you stop thinking of talk as a delay and start treating it as work, your numbers change."

CHAPTER 10

WHAT TO SAY WHEN THEY'RE READY TO TALK

Y OU WILL KNOW WHEN they are ready. It is not subtle.

They stop moving. They ask a direct question. They make a statement about what they want or what they need. They say something that tells you they have been thinking about this — really thinking, not just wandering —and the energy shifts. Something opens up.

When that happens, many salespeople celebrate internally and then immediately make the same mistake: they shift into salesperson mode. The voice changes. The posture changes. They start presenting instead of talking.

The customer feels it. And some of them back off just from that — just from the energy shift. They were ready to talk, and then the person they were talking to turned into someone else.

Do not shift. Stay in the same register you have been in. Calm. Conversational. Interested. The only thing that changes is that the conversation is now a little more specific.

Responding to a direct question.

When a customer asks a direct question — what's the mileage on this one, does this come in four-wheel drive, what's the price — answer it directly. Do not redirect. Do not answer a question they did not ask. Do not qualify the answer with a sales pitch attached.

They asked a question. Answer it. That is the most powerful thing you can do in that moment because it is the least expected. Customers anticipate being redirected. When you just answer the question, you become someone they can trust.

After the answer, you can ask one question back. "Is four-wheel drive something you definitely need, or are you still deciding?" That keeps the dialogue going without turning the exchange into a presentation.

When they tell you what they want.

Some customers, once they warm up, will just tell you. "I need something with third-row seating, my budget is around X, and I'd like to stay under a certain payment."

When a customer does this, resist the temptation to immediately run to inventory. Stay with them for another moment. Confirm what you heard.

"So third-row, budget around X, and payment is the priority over purchase price?"

That one confirmation does a lot. It shows them you were listening. It makes sure you did not miss anything. And it gives them the chance to add something they forgot, which customers constantly do.

Now find them the vehicle. Not three vehicles. The vehicle. The one that fits what they told you. Suppose you have to show them two options, fine. But come back with a direction, not a tour of the lot.

The test drive conversation.

If you are moving toward a test drive, do not make it a production. You are not a flight attendant running through a safety demonstration. You are two people about to go for a drive.

"Let me grab the key, and we'll take it out."

That's it. Simple. Confident. No ceremony.

During the drive, let them drive. Let them feel it. Ask a question or two — "How does this compare to what you're in now?" — but mostly let the vehicle do the work. You have done your job. Now the vehicle does its job.

When they are ready, they will show you.

You do not always have to manufacture the closing moment. Customers who are ready will show you. They will ask about the payment. They will ask whether you can do anything about the price. They will ask what happens next.

When a customer asks, "What does the process look like from here?" — that is not a question. That is a green light.

Recognize it. Move forward. Calmly, confidently, without spiking the energy.

You brought them from "I'm just looking" to here. Finish it the same way you started — by following their lead.

"The Rule: When the customer is ready, they will signal it. Your job at that point is to recognize the signal and respond to it — not to force the moment before it arrives."

Chapter 11

The Biggest Mistakes After the Brush-Off

We discussed in Chapter 2 what salespeople get wrong in their first response. But mistakes do not stop at the first response. Some of the worst ones come later — after the customer has warmed up, after the conversation has started, sometimes even after the customer has basically told you they want to buy.

Here are the ones I have watched kill deals that were already won.

Celebrating too early.

The customer has been on the lot for twenty minutes. The conversation is going well. They are laughing, engaged, and asking good questions. The salesperson starts to feel it — this is going to happen — and something in their energy shifts. They get a little looser. A little more casual. Sometimes a little sloppy.

The customer feels the shift. And sometimes that shift makes them uncomfortable. They were having a conversation with a professional, and now they feel like the professional has already counted the commission. Some of them pull back at that point. Not because the deal was bad. Because the energy got weird.

Stay professional all the way through. Do not celebrate until the paperwork is signed.

Bringing up the price too soon.

The customer is still in the emotional phase of the decision. They are connecting with the vehicle, imagining themselves in it, running it through their mental checklist. And the salesperson, trying to be helpful or trying to qualify them, drops a number on them.

That number takes the customer out of the emotional space and into the analytical one. Now they are running math in their head instead of imagining their commute in this truck. It is very hard to get them back to where they were.

Do not lead with price. Let them fall a little in love with the vehicle first. The price conversation is easier when the customer has already decided they want the thing.

Talking through the customer's decision.

The customer is quiet. They are thinking. And the salesperson, uncomfortable with the silence, fills it.

That is one of the most expensive mistakes in sales.

When a customer goes quiet, they are doing the work: standing next to a vehicle, sitting in it, or looking at numbers. They are deciding. If you interrupt that process with talk — features, reassurances, comparisons, anything — you are pulling them back out of the decision and making them start over.

Let the silence sit. It is not empty. Something is happening in it. Wait.

Overselling after the customer has already decided.

The customer has made their decision. They are ready. And the salesperson, not reading the room, keeps adding things. More features. Another comparison. One more reason why this is the right vehicle.

Each additional reason is a risk. Because now the customer is not just agreeing with you—they are evaluating every new thing you say. And one of those things might introduce a doubt they did not have before.

When the customer is done, stop selling. Transition to the next step. You have already won this part. Move forward.

Letting the customer leave without a plan.

The conversation went well. The customer says they need to think about it. They leave.

The salesperson says, "No problem," and watches them drive away.

That is not a plan. That is hope.

Before a customer leaves — even one who had a good experience and is genuinely thinking it over — you need a next step. Not a hard close. A next step.

"When do you think you'll have a chance to talk it over?"

"If I see something come in tomorrow that fits what you described, is it okay if I give you a call?"

"Would it help if I put together the numbers on this one so you have something to look at tonight?"

Any of those keeps the thread alive. None of them is pressure. They are just professional follow-through from someone who took the customer seriously.

The customer who leaves without a next step is not thinking it over. They are shopping somewhere else.

FROM THE FLOOR

I was sitting in the front lobby of a dealership I managed — with a glass-front wall and a full view of the lot. A car pulled in. Two salespeople inside saw it at the same time. They both jumped up, ran for the door, and literally shoved each other trying to get through it first, pushing and shoving like it was a race.

The customers, still in their car, watched every second of this.

The one who won was out of breath when he got there. He stuck his hand out and started talking before he'd even caught his breath, never looked at the wife, never acknowledged the kids in the back seat. Just started in.

The family looked around for a few minutes and left.

When I asked what happened, the salesperson said: "They were just look-ing."

No. They were watching. And what they watched told them everything they needed to know about what the next hour would feel like. The sprint didn't just cost a deal; it cost a deal. It answered every one of the customer's silent questions about this place — and none of the answers were good.

That story is not about a sprint. It covers every mistake we covered in this chapter, compressed into 90 seconds.

The deal was lost before a single word was spoken. Because the salesperson was operating from the wrong instincts — urgency instead of calm, competition instead of professionalism, talking instead of reading the room.

Get the instincts right. The words take care of themselves.

"The Rule: The deal is lost more often after the brush-off than during it. Stay sharp all the way through. The biggest mistakes come when you think it's already won."

Chapter 12

A Repeatable System for Handling "I'm Just Looking"

Everything in this book comes down to a system. Not a script. A system.

Scripts break down the moment the customer says something unexpected. A system holds because it is built on principles — on understanding what the customer needs at each stage — not on memorized lines.

Here is the system, start to finish.

Step 1: The approach.

Walk out at a normal pace. Not a sprint. Not a slow stroll either — something that says you are a professional who is glad they are here, not someone who is desperate or indifferent. Introduce yourself by name. Shake hands if the moment calls for it. Make eye contact. Smile like you mean it.

One line. That is your whole opening. "Hi, I'm Bruce — glad you came in. What brings you in today?"

Or simpler: "Welcome in. Anything I can help you find?"

Keep it clean. Keep it human.

Step 2: The first response to the brush-off.

They say, "I'm just looking." You say something easy and calm.

"No problem at all. Take your time."

Then you add the door: "If anything catches your eye and you want to take a look inside or take it out, just let me know."

Then you step back. Not inside. Back. Visible, present, not hovering.

That is the whole first response. Fifteen seconds. Done.

Step 3: Read the lot.

Now you watch. Where do they go? How fast are they moving? What are they stopping at? Are they talking to each other? Are they looking back toward you?

You are gathering information. You are not idle. You are doing the most important work in the process right now — learning who this customer is before you say another word.

Step 4: The re-entry.

When the signals say they are ready — they slow down on a vehicle, they look up, they try a door handle, they glance in your direction — you move. Calmly. Toward the vehicle they are at.

You start with something low-stakes. A comment about the vehicle. An easy question. Not a pitch. Not a qualifying battery.

"That's a solid one. What caught your eye about it?"

Let them answer. Follow the answer.

Step 5: The conversation.

One question at a time. Let them talk more than you do. Learn what they actually need. Make it about their life, not about the inventory.

When they are ready to go further, they will show you — offer the next step. Key out of the lot. Walk inside to look at the numbers. Whatever makes sense based on where they are.

Do not push. Follow.

Step 6: The next step — always.

Whether they buy today or leave to think about it, there is always a next step. Always.

If they buy: smooth transition into the process, no spike in energy, stay professional.

If they leave, you have a name, a phone number, and a specific follow-up plan. Not "call me if you have questions." A specific next step. "I'll call you on Thursday to see if you had a chance to look at those numbers."

That is the system. Six steps. None of them is complicated. All of them require discipline — especially the patience in the middle, where most salespeople fall apart.

Run this system on every customer who says, "I'm just looking," and your numbers will change. Not because you said something magic. Because you stopped making the mistakes that were costing you deals.

"The Rule: A system beats a script every time. Know the principles. Apply them to whatever the customer gives you. That's how you handle it every time."

Chapter 13

The "I'm Just Looking" Checklist

Use this before your shift. Use it when you are reviewing a deal that got away. Use it when you are training someone new and trying to show them where things went sideways.

This is the whole system compressed into a checklist. Check every box on every customer, and you will not lose a deal to a brush-off again.

The approach

- ✓ Normal pace — not a sprint, not a crawl
- ✓ Professional appearance before you step outside
- ✓ Introduce yourself by name
- ✓ One clean opening line — no monologue
- ✓ Genuine eye contact and a real smile

The first response

- ✓ Acknowledge the brush-off without flinching
- ✓ Keep the response calm and brief
- ✓ Leave the door open ("just let me know")
- ✓ Step back — do not disappear, do not hover

On the lot

- ✓ Stay visible and accessible
- ✓ Watch where they go and how fast they move
- ✓ Look for the signal that the door is opening

✓ Do not approach again until the signal appears

The re-entry

✓ Move toward them naturally — no announcement

✓ Start with something easy and low-stakes

✓ Ask one question about what they are looking at

✓ Follow their answer, do not redirect

The conversation

✓ One question at a time

✓ Let them talk more than you do

✓ Make it about their needs, not the vehicle's features

✓ Let the silence sit when they are thinking

✓ Do not oversell after they have decided

The close or the follow-up

✓ Recognize the green-light signals

✓ Transition calmly — do not spike the energy

✓ If they leave, always establish a specific next step

✓ Get a name and number before they go

✓ Follow up when you said you would

The mindset

✓ Do not take it personally

✓ Do not assume it is a verdict

✓ Treat every customer like they might be the taxi customer

✓ Stay professional from the first step to the last

That is the whole thing. Not complicated. Requires discipline. Requires patience. Requires you to put the customer's pace ahead of your own instincts.

Do that consistently, and "I'm just looking" becomes the least scary phrase in car sales.

Because you will know exactly what to do when you hear it.

"The Rule: A checklist is only useful if you actually use it. Run through these steps before your shift until they become instinct. Then run it anyway."

CONCLUSION

Why Mastering the Brush-Off Changes Everything

I want to leave you with something simple.

Every salesperson on every lot in this country hears "I'm just looking" every single day. Most of them hear it as a wall. They back off, give up, write the customer off, and move on to the next one.

You now know what it actually is.

It is a request. It is information. It is the beginning of the conversation, not its end. And you have a system — a real, repeatable system — for what to do when you hear it.

That is not a small thing. That is the difference between a salesperson who loses deals in the first thirty seconds and one who converts them.

I have watched salespeople completely transform their results just by fixing this one thing. Not by learning a new closing technique. Not by memorizing better scripts. By understanding what "I'm just looking" actually means and responding appropriately.

The customer who says they are just looking is almost always still in play. They came to the lot. They got out of the car. They are standing there, looking at the vehicles, which means, on some level, they are interested. Your job is not to overcome their resistance. Your job is to remove the pressure that is creating it.

Do that, and the resistance dissolves on its own.

Stay calm. Stay present. Follow their lead. Give them real space without disappearing. Come back at the right moment with something easy. Let the conversation build at their pace. Recognize the green lights. Finish it the same way you started it — without pressure, without urgency, without making it about you.

That is professional car sales. That is what the best people in this business do every day.

Now you know how to do it too.

— *Bruce Huddleston*

Tips For The Sales Manager

If you manage a sales team, the skills in this book are not just for your salespeople to develop on their own. They are something you can build into your culture, your training, and your daily coaching.

Here is how to use what is in this book at the management level.

Watch the first response, not just the result.

Most managers evaluate salespeople on numbers. Closing percentage, units, gross. Those are the outcomes. But the place where deals are most often lost is at the very beginning — in the first thirty seconds after a customer says they are just looking.

Stand at the window. Watch how your salespeople respond to the brush-off. What you see there will tell you more about why the numbers look the way they do than any spreadsheet will.

Use the checklist as a training tool.

The checklist in Chapter 13 is not just for individual salespeople. Run it with your team in your next sales meeting. Go through each item and ask: Do we actually do this? Where are we strong? Where are we leaving deals on the table?

The answers will show you exactly where your training focus needs to be.

Debrief lost deals differently.

When a customer leaves without buying, the typical debrief goes like this: "What happened?" The salesperson says, "They were just looking," and that is the end of it.

Change the question. Ask: "Where did the conversation go sideways?" Walk them back through the approach, the first response, the time on the lot, the re-entry. Find the specific moment where something could have gone differently. That is where the learning is.

Model the behavior yourself.

If you go out on turns or work the floor yourself, your salespeople are watching how you handle it. If you project calm, confidence, and patience when a customer brushes you off, you are teaching without a word. If you push or disappear, you are teaching that too.

Be the example you want your team to follow.

Celebrate patience, not just closes.

Most dealership cultures celebrate the close. The sale. The unit. That is right and appropriate.

But consider also acknowledging the salesperson who handled a difficult brush-off with exceptional patience and professionalism — even if the deal did not close that day. What you celebrate is what you get more of. If you only celebrate outcomes, you will get salespeople who push for outcomes. If you also celebrate process, you will develop salespeople who are worth keeping.

The floor is a classroom. Every interaction is a lesson. Make sure your team is learning the right things from it.

APPENDIX-THE RULES

Every chapter in this book ends with a rule. Here they are collected in one place — the complete system in its simplest form.

Introduction

"The Rule: 'I'm just looking' is not rejection. It is information. Your job is to respond to it — not react to it."

Chapter 1

"The Rule: Don't interpret. Don't assume. Listen to what the phrase is actually telling you and respond to that."

Chapter 2

"The Rule: The most expensive mistake in car sales is making decisions about customers with almost no information. Hold off. Watch. Respond to what you actually see."

Chapter 3

"The Rule: The customer's guard is not the enemy of the sale. It's the gate to it. Respond correctly, and it opens. Push against it, and it locks."

Chapter 4

"The Rule: Acknowledge. Stay. Leave the door open. That's the whole first response. Do not overthink it."

Chapter 5

"The Rule: Stay on the lot. Stay visible. Stay calm. The customer gave you nothing to work with yet — don't give them a reason to leave before they do."

Chapter 6

"The Rule: Re-enter the conversation the way a good friend would — by joining where the customer already is, not by dragging them somewhere they didn't ask to go."

Chapter 7

"The Rule: The customer's feet, pace, hands, and eyes will tell you when the door is open. Watch for the signals and respond to them — not to a timer."

Chapter 8

"The Rule: Sometimes the obstacle is invisible. When the customer is still on the lot, but the conversation keeps stalling, ask yourself what needs to change — not whether you should give up."

Chapter 9

"The Rule: The conversation is the sale. When you stop thinking of talk as a delay and start treating it as work, your numbers change."

Chapter 10

"The Rule: When the customer is ready, they will signal it. Your job at that point is to recognize the signal and respond to it — not to force the moment before it arrives."

Chapter 11

"The Rule: The deal is lost more often after the brush-off than during it. Stay sharp all the way through. The biggest mistakes come when you think it's already won."

Chapter 12

"The Rule: A system beats a script every time. Know the principles. Apply them to whatever the customer gives you. That's how you handle it every time."

Chapter 13

"The Rule: A checklist is only useful if you actually use it. Run through these steps before your shift until they become instinct. Then run it anyway."

Also Available

Also available from Bedrock Heritage Publishing:

The Complete Car Sales Survival Guide

The No-BS Playbook for New Automotive Salespeople

Book 1 — The Meet and Greet Playbook

How to Make Powerful First Impressions with Customers, Clients, and Guests

Book 2 — The First 60 Seconds in Car Sales

A Proven Meet and Greet System to Build Trust and Start More Conversations

Book 3 — How to Handle "I'm Just Looking" in Car Sales

A Simple System to Turn Brush-Offs into Productive Conversations

Book 4 — Body Language in Car Sales

How Posture, Eye Contact, and Presence Build Customer Trust

Book 5 — Greeting Customers on the Lot

How to Approach Buyers Without Pressure

Book 6 — The Ten-Second Rule in Car Sales

Why First Impressions Determine Whether Customers Stay or Leave

Book 7 — The Car Sales Conversation Starter Guide

How to Begin Natural Conversations That Lead to Sales

Book 8 — Car Sales Confidence for New Salespeople

How to Approach Customers Without Fear or Hesitation

Book 9 — Common Car Sales Greeting Mistakes

What Drives Customers Away in the First Minute

Book 10 — The First Five Minutes With a Car Buyer

How to Transition from Greeting to Conversation and Move Toward the Sale

All titles are available on Amazon and through IngramSpark.

For bulk orders and dealership pricing, contact:

info@bedrockheritagepublishing.com

ABOUT THE AUTHOR

Bruce Huddleston spent thirty-five years in the automotive industry, working every level of the business from showroom floor salesperson to finance manager, sales manager, used car manager, and general manager. His career included new-car franchise dealerships, independent used-car operations, and a decade in buy-here, pay-here — giving him a breadth of experience that few in the industry can match.

He began as a high school dropout who needed a job and ended up discovering a profession. He ended as a veteran who had trained hundreds of salespeople, managed multiple departments, and built a reputation for straight talk in an industry that doesn't always reward it.

Since retiring, Bruce has opened a life coaching practice, assists his wife with her mental health therapy practice, and operates Bedrock Heritage Publishing, a division of Life Guidance Consulting LLC, where he writes practical guides for sales professionals across multiple industries.

The Complete Car Sales Survival Guide is his flagship work. The Car Sales Survival Guide Series — a collection of focused training guides on specific sales skills — is built on the same foundation of real experience, honest insight, and zero tolerance for the kind of nonsense that gives sales a bad name.

He lives in Tyler, Texas.

A Quick Favor

If How to Handle "I'm Just Looking" in Car Sales helped you — if it changed how you think about the brush-off, gave you a system you didn't have before, or helped you turn a conversation that would have ended into one that went somewhere — I would appreciate a review.

Reviews on Amazon are how other salespeople find books like this one. A sentence or two about what you got out of it is enough. Honesty is all I ask.

You can simply scan the QR code below.

*https://www.amazon.com/rev
iew/create-review/?asin=197
2179268*

Thank you for reading. Now go use it.

— Bruce Huddleston